Photography by:
Hugo van Lawick, Günter Ziesler, Caroline Weaver,
Jeff Smith, Clem Haagner, Gregory G. Dimijian,
Jonathan Scott, R.D. Estes, Julie Bruton, Hans Reinhard.

ZEBRA FAMILY
Jane Goodall

A MADISON MINI BOOK

Published by Madison Marketing Limited.
Madison Marketing Limited holds the exclusive
license to this edition.
Copyright © 1991 by Neugebauer Rights & Licenses AG., Zurich.
Text copyright © 1991 by Jane Goodall.
All rights reserved.
ISBN 1-55066-018-7

Printed in Canada

Printed on recycled paper

ZEBRA FAMILY

Jane Goodall
ANIMAL SERIES

Photographs selected by
Michael Neugebauer

Madison Marketing Limited

*T*his zebra foal is named Zoro. He is only a few weeks old. His mother, Sara, is one of the five mares who run with the stallion named Nelson. There are three yearlings in this family group, too. They are last year's foals. One of these is Zoro's older sister.

The family moves on, and Sara follows behind Zoro.
When they come to a dusty place, Zoro's mother rolls
– just like a horse.

Suddenly a pack of wild dogs approaches. The zebras stand and watch until the dogs get quite close. Then, when one of the hunters darts towards Nelson, the zebras start to run.

Nelson leads his family in a fast gallop away across the plains. Wild dogs don't hunt zebras very often – they prefer smaller animals. Zebra stallions are very brave. They often attack wild dogs or hyenas who get too close.

When the family stops to graze, Zoro suckles. He butts his mother's flank with his head, trying to make the milk flow more quickly. Then, as she keeps guard, he stretches out flat on his side and sleeps.

After grazing for an hour or so, the stallion, who has never strayed far from the sleeping foal, moves on. Zoro wakes up and follows. The three yearlings in the family begin to play, galloping and kicking up their heels as they chase one another. Zoro watches, but he is not yet old enough to join in.

As they travel on, the grass gets shorter. They are
crossing a wide open plain. There are many
Thompson's gazelles feeding here, and some of the
taller Grant's gazelles. We pass other animals too.
A flock of ostriches. A troop of baboons. And one
huge black rhino with her calf.

Later in the afternoon we join many more zebras around a water hole. One group is only males. They are zebras who have left their family groups and are waiting to get mares of their own.

One of the young males trots towards Zoro's family. He rubs up against Nelson's four year old daughter. But Nelson charges him. The young male quickly gives up and canters away. Nelson will keep the female with him a while longer, but soon he'll lose her to another stallion. She is almost ready to start a family of her own.

Near the end of the afternoon the zebras move towards a river. They know lions sometimes hide near water. After every few steps they stop to listen and sniff the air. At last they start to drink. But suddenly something startles them. They race through the shallow water and away to safety.

When they reach the open plains again the zebras calm down. It is cool now, and Zoro kicks up his heels for joy. Later the zebras will gather together in a big camp again. This is safer – then there are more eyes and ears and noses to sense the presence of lions or hyenas or wild dogs.

By this time the sun is setting. Soon it will be dark.
Zoro will be all right. Sara, his mother, is experienced
and alert. Nelson, his father, is brave. And all the other
members of the family will be there to protect him
during the dark African night.

*J*ANE GOODALL has shared her important discoveries and her love of animals with millions of people around the world through books, films and lectures. She has founded ongoing research and educational institutes on two continents, and is one of the world's most acclaimed naturalists.

The Jane Goodall Institute for Wildlife
Research, Education and Conservation
P.O. Box 41720, Tucson, AZ 85717 U.S.A.

The Jane Goodall Institute — Canada
P.O. Box 3125, Station "C"
Ottawa, Ontario K1Y 4J4 Canada

The Jane Goodall Institute — U.K.
15 Clarendon Park
Lymington, Hants SO41 8AX United Kingdom